MAKING OF A MINDFUL EMPLOYEE

FROM EXISTING IN THE JOB TO LIVING THE JOB

LALITA SANWAL, BHARAT PRASAD

Chennai • Bangalore

CLEVER FOX PUBLISHING
Chennai, India

Published by CLEVER FOX PUBLISHING 2025
Copyright © Lalita Sanwal, Bharat Prasad 2025

All Rights Reserved.
ISBN: 978-93-67073-69-8

This book has been published with all reasonable efforts taken to make the material error-free after the consent of the author. No part of this book shall be used, reproduced in any manner whatsoever without written permission from the author, except in the case of brief quotations embodied in critical articles and reviews.

The Author of this book is solely responsible and liable for its content including but not limited to the views, representations, descriptions, statements, information, opinions and references ["Content"]. The Content of this book shall not constitute or be construed or deemed to reflect the opinion or expression of the Publisher or Editor. Neither the Publisher nor Editor endorse or approve the Content of this book or guarantee the reliability, accuracy or completeness of the Content published herein and do not make any representations or warranties of any kind, express or implied, including but not limited to the implied warranties of merchantability, fitness for a particular purpose. The Publisher and Editor shall not be liable whatsoever for any errors, omissions, whether such errors or omissions result from negligence, accident, or any other cause or claims for loss or damages of any kind, including without limitation, indirect or consequential loss or damage arising out of use, inability to use, or about the reliability, accuracy or sufficiency of the information contained in this book.

|| Samba Sadashiv ||

To

Every employee putting in their best

Pooja Prasad
For everything

Asha Devatwal

Dinesh Prasad

भगवती देवी & Ganga Prasad

Late Nand Kishore
For being the father, mother and guiding light

TABLE OF CONTENTS

- **VII** — INTRODUCTION
- **1** — EMPLOYEE ENGAGEMENT
- **25** — ONBOARDING
- **35** — INDUCTION
- **41** — PERFORMANCE MANAGEMENT
- **65** — EXIT MANAGEMENT: THE OFFBOARDING PROCESS
- **82** — EFFECTIVE EMPLOYEE ENGAGEMENT INITIATIVES
- **96** — REFERENCES

INTRODUCTION

Thank you for showing interest in "Making of a Mindful Employee." This book is created to start a dialogue among professionals and organisations about how positive, healthier workplaces and employee engagement lead to better organisational performance.

Every organisation wants the best talent to join them. In the times of recession and mass layovers there is no dearth of opportunities for talent. Even in Mahabharata, Lord Krishna persuaded King Karna to fight for them. Employees with potential are sought after by everyone. But the question is how to build a loyal and value-adding workforce, retain them, and utilise them for the best?

What lies ahead in the book is a discussion about people management and unlocking the potential each human resource carries within itself. The book also attempts to remind employers that the rise of an organisation must be in consonant with the growth and development of the employees. Otherwise, organisations wouldn't be able to leverage the mental depth, enterprising character and intellectual resourcefulness of an employee, which is more than what their resume says.

The book is divided based on the different phases of the employee life cycle, i.e. Employee Engagement, Onboarding, Induction, Performance Management and Exit Management, which are common to all organisations. However, Employee Engagement initiatives remain an integral function throughout the employee life cycle. One can take away multiple learnings from this book, irrespective of the type of workspace and hierarchy it follows.

An average person spends around 90 thousand hours of their active life working for various organisations[1]. Such a great deal of time and lives of people cannot be put to stress, frustration, disengagement at work and toxic working environments, as that would be an injustice to humankind. Through this book, we reflect on our professional experiences to discuss good practices that, if followed, align employees and management toward a common goal, ultimately leading to the growth of the organisation. **By shifting the perspective from merely existing in the job to living the job makes all the difference, and the benefit lies for everyone.**

Each chapter of the book begins with a few global statistics to draw the attention of the management, stakeholders, and HR (which is an extended office of the management), imploring them to bring a paradigm shift in their approaches towards workforce management.

They have to start believing that the employee is worth more than their experience and skill set; that if they are sincerely mentally engaged in their tasks, they can provide a lot to the organisation. **How wonderful a situation would be if 100s of minds are concerned about your organisation as much as you are.**

The index of an organisation's overall growth should be comprised of parameters such as the strength of tenured employees, attrition rate, ex-employee review, Employee Lifecycle Fulfilment Index (introduced in the chapter of Exit Management), Employee Engagement, etc., and not just revenue figures. The HR professionals should also be perceived as assets and seen through the lens of employee satisfaction and retention, brand building, revenue saved, etc., and not just as a non-revenue generating entities.

This book is intended for the management, HR Professionals, employees and students making humble beginnings in their early careers across the small and big organisations of various kinds to develop employee engagement and healthy human resource utilisation. The book aims to help transform your organisation into a balanced, content, and happy workforce that grows holistically.

We would also like to have a special mention of people, we came across in our respective careers and whose thoughts and management initiatives have impacted lives:

Dr. Ashir Tyagi, IRS (C&CE:1994), a path breaker and visionary senior bureaucrat who exemplified the utilisation and wellbeing of human resources with employee engagement at each level of the workforce. From giving wings to mentoring employees, the endeavours brought beautiful effects in the workspace.

Ms. Ashka Ghatge manages talent acquisition and life challenges in a way that inspires others. Her ideas on development of human resources sets her apart. She personifies strength, character and ethics in every role she takes.

At the end of this book, 9 effective employee engagement initiatives are provided which would be useful to every organisation.

    Happy People Management !

*****

"low engagement costs the global economy $8.8 trillion. That's 9% of global GDP — enough to make the difference between success and a failure for humanity." [2]

"93% say achieving work-life balance is important, 60% said personal lives are more important than professional ones. 57% said that they won't accept a job if it interfered with their work life balance." [3]

"engaged employees require a 31% pay increase to consider taking a job with a different organization; not engaged and actively disengaged employees, on average, want a 22% pay increase to change jobs. 43% of employees seeking a new job when engaged and which increased to 61% when disengaged." [4]

"When asked quiet quitting employees, what would you change about your workplace to make it better? 41% said engagement & culture; 16% said wellbeing and only 28 % said Pay and Benefits" [5]

"Only 10% of employees are asked how they like to be recognized and appreciated. And only 23% of employees strongly agree that they get the right amount of recognition for the work they do. Those who do are four times more likely to be engaged." [6]

CHAPTER 1
EMPLOYEE ENGAGEMENT

Introduction

Our discussion about Employee Engagement (EE) may start from this page, but the essence of Employee Engagement is spreaded in nearly every process of the HR Dept. While discussing, the question comes to mind, when the employee has already been hired by the organisation and doing its job, then, what is this kind of engagement? Is employee engagement all about having fun Friday, team dinners or secret santa like activities, or is there anything beyond these? Why is employee engagement becoming a subject of discussion, more than ever? Answering such questions is very important and one of the reasons we started writing this book.

2. Evolution of Employee Engagement

Before the arrival of the modern finance/software type jobs, most of the jobs were mechanical in nature involving less brain intensive and analytic work. Anybody given some training and time to sharpen skills would get on with the job well. The individuality and exclusivity of an employee would not appear much, making them vulnerable to being replaced and reducing their scope to raise demands for their betterment.

Imagine a country called "Republic X," where there is only one major employer named "ABC Pvt. Ltd.", employing most of the working population. Do you think there would be any competitive pressure on ABC Pvt. Ltd., to bring any reform in the working conditions of employees to retain them or initiate any kind of employee engagement for deeper ties? Rather, due to its monopoly with no fear of losing its workforce to anyone else, it wouldn't have a second thought about firing an employee in return for more profit. In this case, the employees are forced to work, and reforms will not come unless the promoter is empathetic or has a change of heart and wants to improve the lives of the employees or the employees have united for their demands (which is again not a very probable case).

Also, not every organisation is TATA, which introduced shorter working hours, well-ventilated workplaces in industries, a crèche for young mothers, installation of the first humidifiers and fire-sprinklers in India. In 1886, they instituted a pension fund, and in 1895, began to pay accident compensation, long before they became statutory in the west.[7]

Even in the modern times, in response to the continuous tradition of welfare of the workforce by TATA, the employees showcased exemplary efforts during the 26/11 Taj attack in Mumbai. The employees of the Taj hotel placed the safety of guests over their own and in the process, some of them sacrificed their lives. What also came to surface was the recruitment system that hires for character and not for grades; training programmes that not just mentor but also empower employees to take decisions; and a reward programme that recognises employees on a real time basis.[8]

However, as the technology advanced and the Internet arrived, common people were able to convert their ideas into businesses even from the garages of their home. This caused mushrooms of businesses to emerge, generating a sea of employment opportunities. Things started picking up pace and more young people began adopting critical positions. One key aspect of the younger generation is that they have less patience than the previous generations and want to achieve things quicker, on a bigger scale and more efficiently. By now the stakeholders have understood that an efficient workforce can change the fortunes of an organisation, and that they need educated employees to handle their growing operations. Thus, began the competition to get into premium colleges, as a degree was an accepted parameter for judging qualifications.

3. Employee Engagement and its need

In the current times of tough competition and depleting profit margins, efficient and loyal employees are sought in industries all over, making the organisation highly reliant and in a way compelled to connect with its workforce. Where, even if one team member leaves, the time lost in hiring the new appropriate employee and training them definitely hurts the momentum and timeline of the work. Also, the cost of replacement may reach up to 40% higher than the previous employee. [9]

Further, as every business houses scratching margins and wants to extract more in less time with less expenditure on employees, the "revenue per employee," and "employee cost as a part of revenue" are becoming critical factors in the health of a balance sheet. In some cases, employee cost reaches about 50 % of the revenue.[10]

Therefore, attributes such as mindfulness, loyalty, enterprising character, interpersonal skills, and out of the box thinking in the workforce have become huge factors in an organisation's success story and showcases the importance of engagement of the employee into the business.

Let us further understand Employee Engagement with the example of two sales executives Raman and John, with same qualifications and remuneration, working for XY Pvt. Ltd. and UV Pvt. Ltd. respectively, dealing in the same product type.

The prime difference is that Raman's firm doesn't work on employee engagement. They believe in hiring-firing if the employee doesn't perform, as there is no shortage of candidates to join the firm. Whereas, John's firm acknowledges the importance of employee engagement and is supportive towards its employees.

Raman goes on field to sell and generate mediocre sales. He does what he is told and doesn't apply much of his mind proactively towards the organisation's business. During the meetings as well he doesn't have much insights to share and mostly agrees with the bosses to be on their side. He does what it takes to remain in the firm.

Now, John also goes on the field to sell and generate similar mediocre sales. However, John tries to observe why the sales are not going up. What are the issues inhibiting the sales. As per his intellect he also converses with customers to know why they are not choosing their product. He applies different strategies to push sales. It is apparent that John has a sense of responsibility, ownership, loyalty and applies his mind into the job. As he had tried to dig into the business and had interacted with several customers, he presents various of his insights during the meetings. John knows that his firm values the efforts of employees irrespective how small they are and encourages employees to speak up their mind. He knows that the management will welcome his analyses and criticism over a product or strategy for the betterment of the firm, and that such initiatives of employees are also considered during Performance Evaluation and annual salary appraisals. He also observes that his organisation tries to enrich his work life balance through various initiatives, perks and benefits. Therefore, in return, John explores his enterprising character and tries to add value to the organisation through his work.

On the other hand, what Raman doing was robotic work with non-application of mind and without much thought given into the job. In conclusion, John is a mindful, satisfied, loyal and engaged employee. **Raman might be existing in the job, but it is John living the job.** In the long run, John's firm (UV Pvt. Ltd.) with the help of ground insights, value addition by employees, experience of tenured employees and feedback from customers would be able to draw better strategies and may outgrow Raman's firm (XY Pvt. Ltd.).

If you do not have to wait or push employees for inputs, if employees are not just physically but mentally present in the office by adding value, applying their minds during work, and taking up proactive measures for the betterment of organisation, then, congratulations, your workforce is akin to a John-like employees.

When the employee is correctly engaged and involved in organisation's business, they not only evolves their own professional personality but compliments the growth of the organisation as well. The lack of an employee engaging culture harms both the employee and their employer. We cannot even measure the loss of productivity in terms of revenue, time & innovations, the disengagement causes. At the same time, it is unfair to the disengaged employees, as they misses out on professional gains by not strongly connected to work.

4. Deriving Employee Engagement

With the above discussion, it is clear that the reliance of organisations on its employees for handling business demands, changing trends and competition is increasing. At the same time restricting the rate at which employees leave the organisation, that is, employee attrition, is important too. This is how Employee Engagement comes into play. In simpler terms we can describe the Employee Engagement as following:

> *Employee Engagement (EE) = Satisfied Employee (SE) + Mindful Employee (ME), in an organisation*
>
> *(Where the value of SE or ME cannot be equal to Nil)*

(i) **Satisfied Employee (SE)** - An employee is satisfied through various means such as perks, benefits, fair performance evaluation, conducive work culture, promotional aspects, strong grievance management, fair compensation, personal and family wellbeing. Such factors also balance the work and personal life of an employee by allowing them to focus on work.

(ii) **Mindful Employee (ME)** - This condition is fulfilled when the employee who is hired for their skills, degree and work experience, not just completes the assigned tasks but also mindfully engages in the workplace. A mindful employee utilises their intellect, experience and mental depth to bring out of the box solutions, uses creative approaches and initiatives for reforming the regular assigned work. The employee will also acknowledge ownership of the work and provide inputs for the organisation. All this happens when the employee is mentally engaged through various effective engaging initiatives.

When an organisation has the employee satisfied, they may be turned into mindful employees leading to increased Employee Engagement.

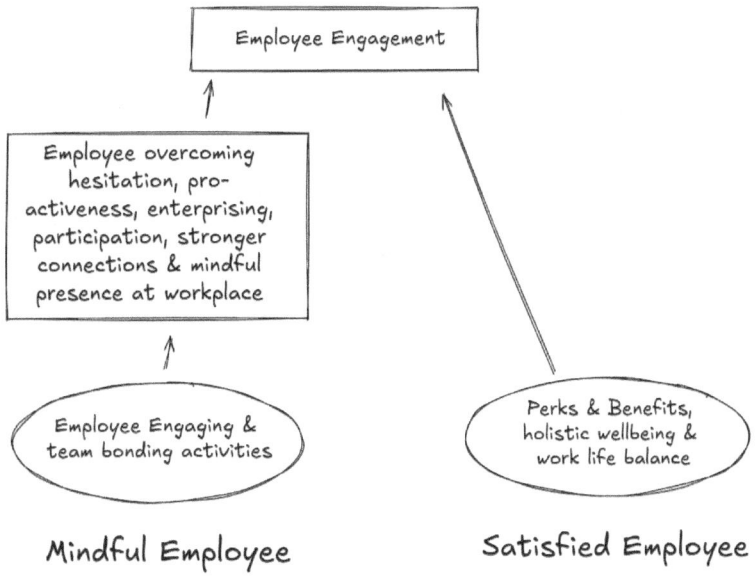

[Fig. 1] Employee Engagement

5. Employee Engaging Activities

What are these

Employee Engaging activities are about making the employee more mindful towards the job and its responsibilities. **Such mindfulness comes through regular effective interactions and supportive dialogue of the manager with the employee and thus directing the mental capacity and energy of the employee for productive and constructive efforts.**

It is very crucial that manager interact and discuss the work with the employee on a regular basis, allowing the employee to open up with their mindset, findings/shortcomings in the workflows, tasks, strategies and proposals or any other personal issues. Such exercises will evolve a sense of ownership, making them more mindful and help integrate employee in the organisation.

The benefit lies for the managers as well, as they must know what each employee is invested in and how are they progressing with the task. A manager not knowing what employees are up to is the inefficiency on managers part and not the employees.

A component of employee engagement also includes group activities such as team dinners, movies, outings, sport matches and other development activities. The idea behind is that putting people in a team is one thing and making them work together is another. People who eat, play, and have fun together, stay connected and also tend to work more cohesively. Such activities focus on team bonding, team building and bridging the mental gaps between team members. They also break the monotony of work and induce fresh air into the office atmosphere.

What they do

Employee Engagement ultimately aim to initiate the employee towards mindfulness and breaking the hesitation, an individual team member carries within themselves. It reduces the mental and emotional distance between the employees, team members, managers and creates space for spending time with each other and therefore, gradually one starts understanding the thought process of the other person. The gains from the activities are reflected in teamwork.

We believe that most people are good human beings having their own side of stories, compulsions and baggage that pushes them to do or be who they are. They may seem indifferent and awkward from a distance but when communication is set up and people come close, the understanding between them increases. Fun Fridays, team outings, secret santa, sports competitions, etc., are just a few tools and a small part of employee engagement to bring employees closer.

However, the success of such group activities depends on the involvement of the managers and how much are they willing to have an engage workforce. Ideally, the managers should take a lead and encourage the employee to be part of such activities.

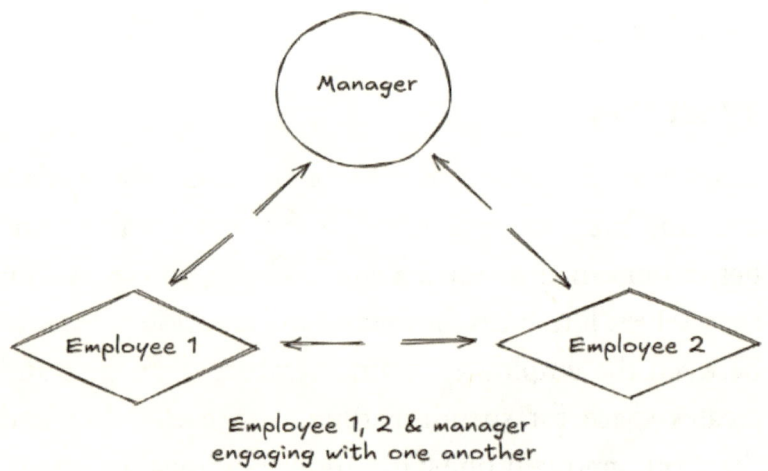

Employee 1, 2 & manager engaging with one another

[Fig. 2] Employee - Manager Engagement

As when a solid object melts into liquid, it loses its shape and identity. During this process, the entropy i.e. the randomness of molecules increases. By infusion of Employee Engagement, we intend to decrease the entropy (considering the molecules as employees), so that the solid (the organisation) doesn't lose its shape and identity but on the contrary gets more solidified and strong.

Indian Army - An Epitome of Employee Engagement

A team bonded together can work with greater efficiency towards a common goal. We must learn from the excellent functioning of the Indian Army. The army accomplishes even the most difficult missions only because each team player plays its part and provides substantial inputs to the team. By keeping up together day and night, participating in various exercises and missions, sharing the highs and lows, the lives of the army personnel delve into each other. They develop excellent synergy and understanding within the team and thus, deliver on impossible tasks. What can be a bigger example than a person dedicating its life while protecting its team members and defending the nation. It is the epitome of team bonding and fulfilment of responsibilities one has towards their organisation.

In addition, the culture of the army cultivates practices where officers lead from the front and prioritise the well-being of their colleagues and fellow soldiers. This is a lesson every organisation should apply.

6. The necessity

With the above discussion, we have brought employee engagement under focus. Now the next task is to value and consider what the employee says.

Employees in all sorts of industries who work on ground zero interact with the client and customers, come across real issues and predicaments. These are the people who sell and handover the final product produced after investing a chunk of money into R&D. They might not think holistically as in the seat of a CEO, but they know the most on ground. What should or could have been done? Why are footfalls not converting into real sales? What were the actual reasons for delay in project deliveries? What went wrong with the client and could've been improved during the year long IT project? Why is production not reaching the optimum levels? Which HR policy makes no impact on the employee and is a waste of money for the organisation? They take real-time feedback.

Doesn't matter how much organisations try to take the after sales service feedback, it cannot match with the raw moments of frustration or satisfaction the client/customer has had with the employee. In short, the observations, inputs and critical insights received by the employees, if channelled correctly may change the future course of actions, design of a product or policy. Such organic inputs empower the stakeholders to draft effective strategies, in the absence of which they would be less equipped to do so. Therefore, these employees are not just a part of the executive machinery, but also, indirectly contribute a lot to the decision-making bodies.

When the stakeholders prepare policies for everyone from top to bottom, they must also have inputs from bottom to top. The CEO and the management might look very powerful, but they all can function only if they know their organisation, markets and on ground reality thoroughly, for which they must have reports made up of feeds and inputs from every level of the organisation. Therefore, it is of great importance that employees speak up and mindfully engage in the organisation's business.

In a meeting, if an employee is able to put forward their thoughts and positive-negative criticism about work and organisation without any reluctance, then the organisation must realise that they have got the nectar of employee engagement and the HR policies are working in the right direction. The employee has to be engaged at every phase of the employee life cycle. The methods may alter, but the motive remains the same to make the employee more mindful and engaged in the business.

The time has come for both the employee and employer to understand that the 2nd most valuable part during the hiring of an employee is their resume. The 1st most important thing is the Mind, which has the intellect to observe, analyse and enterprise. Anybody can gain years of experience, and eventually everyone will. Skills can also be learned and taught or may be replaced by technology. However, the only

thing which cannot be replaced is the engagement of employees' mind and the valuable output coming out of it.

7. The culture of Engaging the Employee

When we find something engaging, we remain mentally attached to it and regularly update ourselves with the latest information. For example, in a sports match, we not only regularly update ourselves with the score, but also give our views on strategies that could have been adopted by the team.

In a conducive and employee engaging work culture, the employees see their own development in the growth of the organisation. They will be more focused on work, satisfied and mindful at the workspace. Subsequently, it will also promote a good name of the organisation, attracting new talents and building a brand.

One of the major objective of employee engagement is to impart the sense of ownership of work to the employee. In such a culture, the management has to elevate the prominence of employees at each level and introduce the vision of the organisation as if it is the employee's vision. The short- and long-term goals should also be shared with the employees in a comprehensive way and make them realise that they have a purpose in their work. They should be made connected with various developments in the organisation. An employee must feel a sense of authority and know how their tasks benefit the organisation in getting close to the goals.

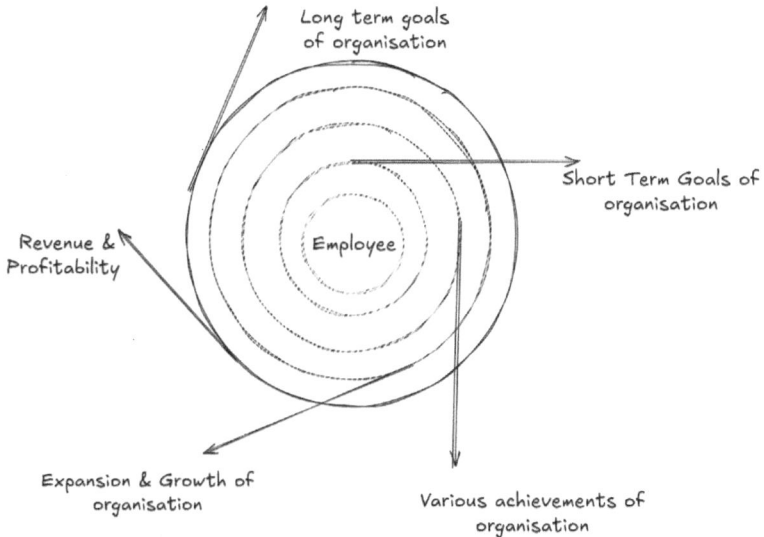

[Fig. 3] Employee being the centre of developments in the organisation

A culture may be grown where employees who compromise their personal lives for the organisation or go that extra mile to help others achieve their goals are appreciated. The little achievements and the critical issues resolved by an employee should not wait for any occasion to be applauded. Further, employees working on something new must be encouraged even if things didn't go as expected. As at the end of the day, they are supporting the organisation. This would also motivate the rest of the employees.

As part of the employee engagement, the employee has to be seen in association with their family and it should be reflected in policies of the organisation. The manager should know their team members and a brief about their background and how something at a personal level affects their behaviour and performance. As part of culture, at a time when the employee is sick or is in critical condition, the team members and management must come forward for assistance and keep in touch with the family. Once this element is roped in, it leaves a significant impact on the employee as well as on their family. It is also important as the concept of nuclear family dominates our modern family structures, therefore, in case of any big mishap, people in current times find themselves at a vulnerable position.

With all the above mentioned endeavours, this book intends, integration of an employee's mind into the organisation's processes and business to increase the productivity. **Modification in the approach and focus of the employee from mere existing in the job to living the job.** Therefore, the issues which make a sincere, efficient and aspiring employee feel uncomfortable, depressed and unhappy to come to the office, must be investigated by the management as a priority.

In simpler terms, Employee Engagement is about organisations addressing the issues and concerns related to employee's personal and professional wellbeing. In return they seek engagement and sincere focus from the employee towards the work.

7. Grievance Management

Employees, managers and anyone who participates at the workplace have to understand that professional etiquettes are not just limited to greetings and other pleasantries but also exhibiting their best while guiding someone through the work and rectifying mistakes.

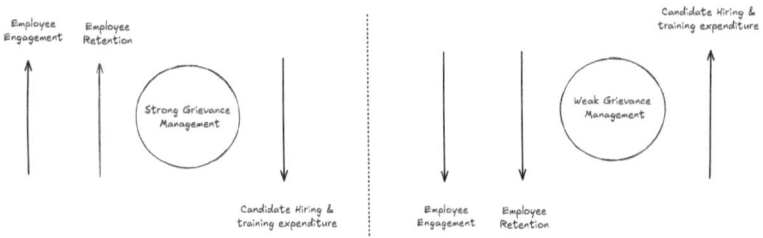

[Fig. 4] Grievance Management

This brings us to another major component which keeps employees confident about their employer is having an active, empathetic and neutral Grievance Management Cell. It is a space for employees to discuss and vent out their experiences and emotions in the event of being misbehaved, humiliated and targeted at the workspace.

8. The Soft Scrutiny

Another feature which organisations may introduce is evaluation of managers by employees. Although, it is desired by most employees, it can create some unfortunate circumstances wherein managers are bound by the review system and cannot exercise administration effectively. This would hamper the workflow, resulting in managers not able to meet targets. However, some soft parameters outlining the organisational policies such as the following may be brought into the system which will not inhibit the managerial work but bring some soft scrutiny over managers for their proper alignment with the company policies and creating a conducive environment:

(i) How effective has the manager been in making the employee utilise organisational benefits, perks and other schemes?

(ii) How effective has the manager been in promoting work life balance as per organisation's policies?

(iii) How effective has the manager been in controlling biases and partiality in the team?

(iv) Does the employee feel comfortable discussing work related issues with the manager?

Such a practice will empower employees and encourage managers to be alert, aware and ensure adherence to organisational policies and guidelines thus, enhancing the employee engagement.

9. Work Anxiety and Continuous Communication

Work anxiety is another issue in our workplaces and almost everyone has faced that sensation of anxiety in their mind and body. Sometimes, it is due to a significant event, but often it occurs due to inappropriate timelines, unfair work distribution, toxic work culture, job security, not being connected to the manager and weak grievance management.

Another key reason that has aggravated the symptoms of work anxiety is the arrival of mobile phone chat applications, which keeps everyone connected 24x7. Anxiety is a mental issue and like every machine, our mind also requires time off from work. With messages sent even after work hours (with the assumption that a message sent is seen), never lets our mind switch off from office space to personal wellbeing. It feeds the mind with constant updates, instructions and urgent work, for the next day. Many times, such messages and their acknowledgement by the employee build up to longer chats consuming the personal time. It is not only disturbing their personal relationships but causing long term effects on their health as well. This hinders in accomplishing the "Satisfied Employee" component we discussed above. A regulation introduced in 2024 by Australia that allows employees to ignore work communications after their official work hours, and with many European countries already having such provisions in place, further emphasises the significance of the issue. [11]

What we need here is understanding the importance of recharging ourselves after office hours with personal wellbeing, by spending time on oneself, family and friends, so that we can begin the next day with better emotional and cognitive health.

The challenge for all of us is to collectively learn to prudently separate the very important critical information from the important or regular ones and utilise mobile platforms more wisely.

10. Perks and Benefits (P&B)

P&B policies play an important role in establishing employee engagement. If an employee planning to resign, but think twice because of the P&B policies then it should be understood that they have served their purpose. These should be developed considering the diversity, needs and requirements of the employees.

Some organisations may have employees with an average age of 25 years while some may have 40 years, also in some female employees can outnumber male, therefore, such scenarios should be taken into account.

Few examples of perks are discounts at selective outlets, work or birth anniversary vouchers, club memberships, in house breakfast-lunch, flexible working hours, performance bonus, international or domestic trips, etc. Perks are not statutory and they can be short term, long term or one time and can be changed as per business requirements and management decisions.

However, benefits are essentially a part of the salary package that is offered to a candidate at the time of joining. Benefits have more of a permanent nature and can be revised with the latest market trends. Few examples are subsidised medical insurance for the employee's family, leave encashment policy, referral bonus program, subsidised monetary loan, and service awards.

> *As Plato said "the beginning is the most important part of the work." The next chapter is Onboarding, which is also the beginning of the employee lifecycle.*

*****

"88% of employees believe they are not given a good onboarding program." [12]

"34% of employees have not witnessed any onboarding program at their organization." [13]

"At Microsoft, 56% of new hires who met with their onboarding buddy at least once in their first 90 days indicated that their buddy helped them to quickly become productive in their role. That percentage increased to 97% for those who met more than eight times in their first 90 days." [14]

"Great employee onboarding gives companies a 2.5x revenue growth and 1.9x profit margin compared with organizations with poor onboarding." [15]

CHAPTER 2
ONBOARDING

The first phase of the employee life cycle is called Employee Onboarding. It is the period between a candidate accepting the job offer and them starting to work for the organisation as an employee.

The onboarding phase may seem to occupy very less duration in the complete employee life cycle, but is significant for paving a successful path for a newly joined employee. Within the Onboarding, the Pre-onboarding process, as the name suggests, precedes the actual Onboarding on the organisation's turf.

2. Pre-Onboarding

Pre-onboarding begins when the candidate submits their acceptance to the job.

Here, the HR initiates the joining process by asking them for important documents such as IDs, educational certificates, address proof, bank account details, payslips, experience letters, etc. With this information, the database and the Human Resource Information Management System (HRIMS) portal of the organisation is updated and a new account for the employee is created.

Now comes majorly two type of scenarios:

a. The candidate is a fresher or currently not employed and can join the organisation immediately, therefore, onboarding may be initiated at the earliest.

b. The candidate is already employed and has to serve the notice period at their current organisation. In this case, the pre-onboarding may be initiated prior to the joining date. If the candidate is relocating, pre-onboarding may be initiated a few days before their journey to the new office location.

3. Onboarding

The Onboarding process begins on the first day of the employee in the organisation. They are welcomed with a kit (known as the welcome kit) and go through the document verification process. Generally, the process of onboarding involves providing working infrastructure, workstation, and a walking tour of the workspace (locating the pantry, restrooms, conference room, etc). A brief introduction to different team members is also provided. After that, the employee is asked to go through the employee handbook before the Induction process begins. The background verification is generally initiated once the documentation of the candidate is completed. A chronological checklist of processes and documentation may be designed for ease of working.

4. Mindful Onboarding

The first interaction of the candidate as an employee is crucial, as it is going to leave a lasting impression on them. The management and HR must explore various ways to improve the employee onboarding experience and utilise this as an opportunity to initiate employee engagement at the beginning itself.

To begin, the process of Pre-onboarding is an occasion for the organisation to start building a bond with the candidate. As the candidate has accepted the offer, the recruiter/ HR should remain in touch with the candidate (not overdoing it) to convey that they can reach out whenever in need. This also helps in imparting a sense that the organisation has a concerning culture towards employees. The HR may enquire about any assistance required in case the candidate is moving to a new location either themselves or along with their family.

4.2 Employee & Family

An employee hired from a different location, remains mentally occupied in settling down for the initial days. We should not just look after its onboarding in the organisation, but also extend the helping hand for adjustment of family in the new city. The faster the settlement, the sooner the employee will be able to focus on work. While the employee in need would reach out to the HR for assistance, but what truly makes a difference is that someone from the organisation proactively shows concern for the needs of the new employee. Such little things stay in mind and heart. There is no greater relief than help coming at the right moment. This will give the employee an impression that they have joined a good organisation where valuing employees is not just on paper. This may sound overwhelming to the HR, but the management should attempt to establish a culture of lending a helping hand in the organisation. Such a culture ignites the employee's engagement tendencies at the beginning itself and also promotes a culture of bonding among employees. The benefitted employees would share their experience with other potential candidates and therefore, these initiatives help organisations to create a strong and attractive workplace. In fact, a digital **Welcome Guide** that is regularly updated with relevant information on nearby establishments such as hospitals, schools, recommended doctors, travelling modes, brief about the city, good restaurants to try, important markets and places, trusted real estate agents, contacts for emergency, etc., may be created and shared with the new employee. This guide should have major content recommended "by the employees for the employees" and must not be merged with the organisation employee handbook. This will effectively help the new employee and their family to smoothly settle down.

4.3 A Mindful Reception

A healthy and warm welcome gives the message of a promising relationship. For example, consider an employee not being greeted and attended properly on their very first day at the office. They are asked to wait and meanwhile they struggle to find what to do next, resulting significant loss of time. They may perceive that their presence doesn't affect the place. Everyone is busy amongst themselves and things are not well managed, making the employee feel less valued. They may draw a comparison between their past employer and new organisation. Now, the first impression of the organisation has been created and if things do not improve soon, the negativity in the mind of the employee will persist. A bad onboarding affects the employee mentally, which takes time to overcome.

Such are the triggering points for employee disengagement and once the employee starts feeling disengaged, they would not be able to think beyond the point of remuneration in return of work and merely existing in the job. They will be least interested in the growth of the organisation.

Instead, if they had been treated well with attention, and the HR had prepared for their visit in advance and managed things in a better way, the candidate would have looked forward to starting work and giving their best. The initial interaction should elevate the employee experience and the new joiner should always be greeted with a warm and welcoming body language of the HR. A simple task such as offering water or tea-coffee and complementary lunch must be included. The connection between the two should be generic and approachable, which should make the new joiner comfortable.

The HR must timely share the date of joining and other relevant details of the candidate with the IT support team. A personalised welcome kit (a bunch of useful accessories such as pen, diary, t-shirt, notepad, bottle, etc.,) and other accessories such as ID card may be arranged. The new employee will feel elated with everything arranged on their arrival. It also gives the impression that the organisation was preparing for the employee and looking forward to working with them. Similarly, a floor walk might seem very trivial, but it is a good tool to make the employee feel comfortable around the place. Likewise, during the form fill-up and documentation, the HR department must engage patiently with the employee. Even if the employee feels difficulty in understanding or makes some oversights, the HR should patiently explain and correct things.

Such intentions and efforts of the HR influences the new employee in every small way and sets the tone, be it their energy or excitement level. **Our efforts should be directed at treating the employee like a new asset that the organisation has acquired and make the onboarding process easy and impressive for the employee.** All we need is a change in our perception of welcoming new talent into the organisation.

> *Each employee has earned the job after clearing a number of rounds of interviews that is designed by the organisation. Therefore, every employee deserves to be fairly treated.*

4.4 Welcome Buddy

Many organisations have a "Buddy" or "Mentor" Programme which helps the new joiner throughout their onboarding process. Ideally, the buddy is someone from the team where the new employee is going be deputed.

The buddy acts as the go-to person for the new employee. By having an experienced employee to address the technical and general queries of the new employee and provide guidance until the new employee is fully integrated with the processes and grow alongside the organisation, relieves the managers of extra work to some extent. This exercise makes the onboarding effective and also develops the leadership skills of the employee assigned as the buddy.

Onboarding is an ongoing process and must not be treated like a one-day document verification procedure. We need to take regular feedback from the newly joined employee and their manager to understand the gaps in the process and if they require any additional support.

Once the new employee is dissolved into the organisation's culture and gains the trust of the manager, that's when onboarding is completed. In some cases, even after completing the probation, both the manager and the new employee need HR's intervention to help them align with the organisation's objectives and require training and counselling.

> To further strengthen the foundation of the new employee a good induction is also required, which is discussed in the next chapter.

*****

"91% of new hires who received an effective introduction to company culture training feel connected to their workplace - compared to just 29% who say their onboarding experience was lacking." [16]

CHAPTER 3
INDUCTION

Welcome to the Induction

Ideally, Induction is introducing the organisation to the new employee. It may be treated as a part of the ongoing onboarding process which continues till the employee is not effectively integrated into the organisation.

2. Induction programme is more about assimilation and right positioning of the employee in the organisation. For this to happen, the alignment of the employee with policies, structure, ethos & values, work culture, perks &

benefits and other aspects are also critical along with the core working skills of the employee. In fact, an employee aligned with organisational policies and core skills is a greater asset and less burden than an employee with core skills but not aligned with the organisational policies.

3. What happens in an Induction

During the induction, the HR explains and discusses the business of the organisation, employee policies, performance management system, appraisal cycle, leave structure, protocol and guidelines to be followed. It is also an opportunity for the employee to clear up any query and gain better understanding of working culture.

The information about key personnel, such as directors and department heads, may be included to provide insight into the organisation's beginning, background and growth. The induction process is more effective when employees have gone through the employee handbook, as it offers a foundational understanding of the organisation.

4. A Good Induction

In a good induction, the employee is able to absorb the information laid out by the HR, which will make their upcoming life at the office easier. They would be able to concentrate at work, utilise the perks & benefits correctly and not get entangled in adherence to the organisational policies, thus, making the exercise of Induction successful. After all, the same employee is going to work for the organisation and contribute to generating the revenue.

The employee should be encouraged and made comfortable enough to be able to express their opinions and raise questions about any topic. **It is convinced that Induction has to be engaging and a two-way act. It should never be just reading out the presentation to the employee.** If one is doing so, then the methods ought to be changed. If employees are not asking questions or queries during the Induction, then the HR must introspect their methods of conducting the Induction. How can employees have nil doubts about an entirely new organisation?

The HR should present the organisation's expectations and work culture to the employee during the induction. This will support the employee in preparing the mindset required for existing in the organisation. The employee's view on the various aspects and policies should also be sought and at the same time they may also be allowed to discuss the practices at their past employer. This will also give the HR access to a fresh view of practices prevalent in the industry as well as their own standing.

A brief understanding of internal departments and how they work with each other and support the business should also be introduced during the induction. This insight will help the employees to be more connected and understand the real objective behind completing a task and the correct way to do it. Further, live demos of applying leaves and overtime, adjusting late logins, and other tasks on the HRMIS portal, exposing the employees with the system and enhancing their adaptability may also be included. To make the induction effective and increase employee's attention, an assessment test may also be introduced at the end to figure out any areas that need improvement.

The culture of asking questions in organisations should be encouraged. Even silly questions are worth being asked, because, if they can come to one mind, they can come to others as well.

5. After a satisfactory induction, the employees are introduced to their line manager and team. As part of the induction and onboarding process, catch-up calls are scheduled to check if an employee is getting proper training and support by the team.

> *Further, the performance and work of the employee will be assessed by a performance management system laid out in the next chapter.*

"$2.4 million to $35 million a year is lost working hours for an organization of 10,000 employees to take part in performance evaluations." [17]

"Organizations' top three Performance Management priorities are helping employees align work with organizational needs and priorities (49%), helping managers hold employees accountable for achieving performance expectations (46%), and helping employees learn and grow (35%)." [18]

"89 % of HR leaders believe career paths at their organizations are unclear for many employees." [19]

"A mere 22% of employees strongly agree that their performance review process is fair and transparent." [20]

CHAPTER 4
PERFORMANCE MANAGEMENT

Introduction and Evolution

The worst thing an organisation can do to a fine working employee is not give them a fair and accurate evaluation of the work they have done. The after-effects of an unfair evaluation not only affect the employee professionally, but personally as well in the form of salary appraisals, promotional prospects, family disposable income, aspirations, travel and investments. Thus, performance evaluation is a very critical subject. A wrong evaluation will cause greater loss to the organisation than to the employee concerned, as this causes the right employee to leave and the wrong to be promoted. To arrest such errors and infuse transparency in the organisation, the prevalence of performance management is gradually increasing in industries all over. As the name suggests, it analyses and manages the performance of an employee.

The Harvard Business Review [21] draws a brief insight into the evolution of performance management-appraisal-accountability.

A Talent Management Time Line

The tug-of-war between accountability and development over the decades.

ACCOUNTABILITY FOCUS
DEVELOPMENT FOCUS
A HYBRID "THIRD WAY"

■	**WWI**	The U.S. military created a merit-based rating system to flag and dismiss poor performers.
■	**WWII**	The Army devised forced ranking to identify enlisted soldiers with the potential to become officers.
■	**1940s**	About 60% of U.S. companies were using appraisals to document workers' performance and allocate rewards.
■	**1950s**	Social psychologist Douglas McGregor argued for engaging employees in assessments and goal setting.
■	**1960s**	Led by General Electric, companies began splitting appraisals into separate discussions about accountability and growth, to give development its due.
■	**1970s**	Inflation rates shot up, and organizations felt pressure to award merit pay more objectively, so accountability again became the priority in the appraisal process.
■	**1980s**	Jack Welch championed forced ranking at GE to reward top performers, accommodate those in the middle, and get rid of those at the bottom.
■	**1990s**	McKinsey's War for Talent study pointed to a shortage of capable executives and reinforced the emphasis on assessing and rewarding performance.
■	**2000**	Organizations got flatter, which dramatically increased the number of direct reports each manager had, making it harder to invest time in developing them.
■	**2011**	Kelly Services was the first big professional services firm to drop appraisals, and other major firms followed suit, emphasizing frequent, informal feedback.
■	**2012**	Adobe ended annual performance reviews, in keeping with the famous "Agile Manifesto" and the notion that annual targets were irrelevant to the way its business operated.
■	**2016**	Deloitte, PwC, and others that tried going numberless are reinstating performance ratings but using more than one number and keeping the new emphasis on developmental feedback.

♡ HBR

[Fig. 5] Evolution of Performance Management System

2. Functioning of Performance Management System

The Performance Management System (PMS) dissects, analyses and then evaluates the work being done by an employee in a short period of time of 1/2/3 months, but having ramifications to a larger period such as an appraisal cycle. It not only aims to bring out the fair assessment of the employee's performance but also apprises the organisation about how much the employees are fulfilling their Key Responsibility Areas (KRAs) and Goals under various categories measured through Key Performance Indicator (KPIs).

Following are some broad generic parameters involved in tracking the overall performance of an employee in PMS:

Sr. No.	Parameter	Description
1.	**Meeting work timelines**	Assessing the employee performance based on completing the tasks on time.
2.	**Receptiveness to Managerial Feedback**	Assessing the employee's attitude to acknowledge the feedback provided and their ability to work on it for improvements.

3.	Effective Communication	Evaluates the effectiveness of employee's communication with team members and other stakeholders, encompassing both verbal and written forms
4.	Improvement, Change & Ideas proposed	Acknowledging the employee's ideas and efforts towards the improvements, innovations and the development of the organisation.
5.	Exemplification of Leadership Attributes	Measures application of leadership and sense of ownership put in by the employee into work.
6.	Proficiency in Time Management and Task Prioritization	Assesses how efficiently the employee manages the workload and responsibilities to produce desired output.

Also, in continuation of the above parameters, an illustration of PMS working is provided in following table:

Category	Goal	Timeline	Key Performance Indicator	PMS Rating
Sales	Increase quarterly sales by 20%.	End of Q1	Total sales revenue.	Top rating, if employee's total revenue sales is increased by 20%
Customer Service	Improve customer satisfaction by 10%.	Monthly	Customer feedback surveys.	Top rating if customer satisfaction improves by 10%.
Productivity	Reduce order processing time by 15%.	Monthly	Average time taken to process orders.	Top rating if average order processing time is reduced by 15%

| Employee Development | Dedicates 15 hours to self-development courses. | Bi-Monthly | Number of training hours completed by employees. | Top rating if employee dedicates 15 hours to self-development course in 2 months |

[Table 1]

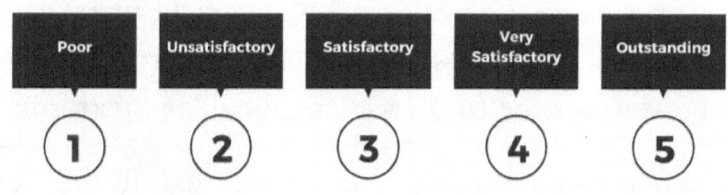

[Fig. 6] Sample Rating in PMS

In the functioning of PMS, the goals are set at the beginning with timelines as per the KRAs of the employee. A Key Performance Indicator is used to scale the output or the goal accomplished. Therefore, if the goal is achieved completely, the highest rating may be given and accordingly, the ratings are decreased with decline in accomplishments.

3. Designing of PMS

An organisation has to design the PMS for itself as per its vision, objectives, nature of work and role of an employee. However, before going into the realm of PMS, every organisation may confront the following questions:

1. Why do we want to implement a PMS and what made us think in this direction?
2. What are the areas of improvement the new PMS is going to address in a better way than the existing performance review system? What are the major gaps?
3. Does the current assessment system inform about the areas where the employees are not able to perform?

The organisation must also ensure that if the performance is going to be evaluated in shorter periods such as monthly or bi-monthly, the PMS to be implemented should be short, crisp and not laborious. A lengthy PMS requiring the employee to be descriptive and provide plenty of feedback will be time consuming. Eventually, it will evolve into a separate task, making the employee lose enthusiasm in the longer run. This can become a concern and backfire.

4. Implementing PMS

The PMS can be implemented in various formats and must be designed as per the organisations' hierarchy, structure and needs. However, two commonly used ones are the 180 and 360 degrees, with little modifications as per the organisation.

180 degree: The 180 degree format works in a way that the employee evaluates its own performance and gives rating to themselves.

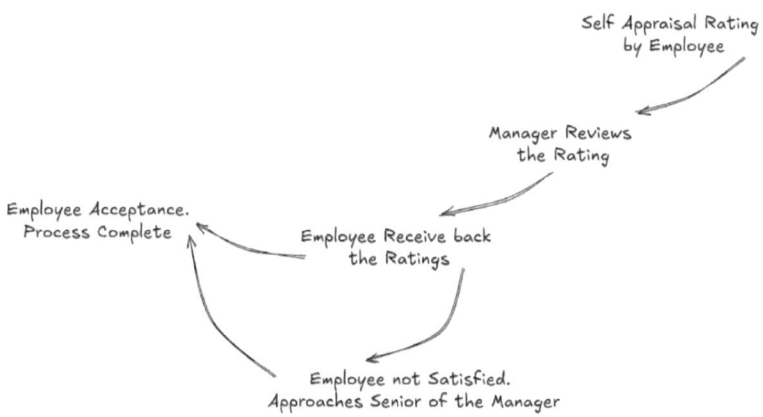

[Fig. 7] 180 Degree PMS flow chart

They then submit the self-evaluation to their manager, who then reviews it and submits back to the employee with its own modifications in rating, if any, along with the feedback. If the employee is satisfied, the process is closed, in case not, the employee approaches the superior of their line manager for resolution.

360 degree: The 360 degree format is more complex with multiple review sources. To understand, consider a managerial level employee working in the sales department. In this job, the employee would have to interact with its seniors, juniors, marketing and operations team, supply chain department, and have to manage sales executives and 3rd party authorised dealers of the organisation. Now, the way employee operates will affect the functioning and coordination of the sales department with other sections. Its working will also influence the relationship of the organisation with the authorised dealers, which is not only critical but will ultimately affect the sales figure and customer relationship.

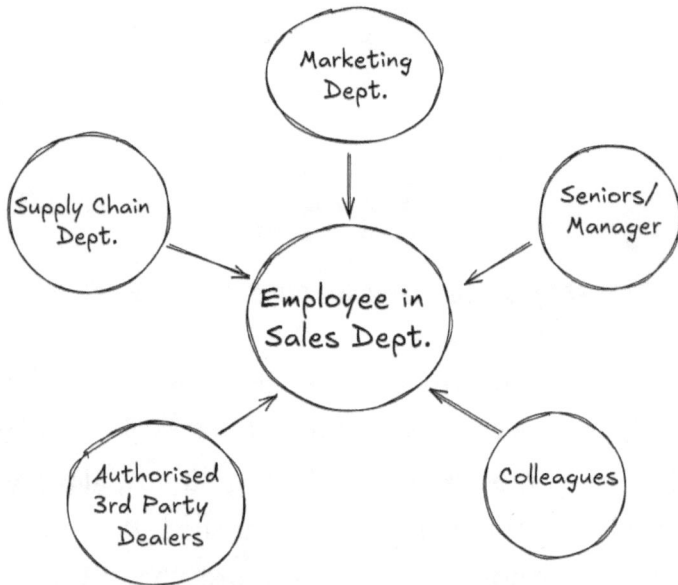

[Fig. 8] 360 Degree PMS flow chart

With this, it becomes pertinent to analyse the working of such an employee from a 360 degree point of view, therefore, the feedback from various sources helps in analysing the behaviour, management and performance aspects of the employee. Further, organisations utilise this format at the time of promoting someone to a senior role, as this format informs how the employee has been handling work at various important positions.

5. PMS & Employee Engagement

As the employees themselves participate in the PMS along with their managers, they become part of the periodic performance evaluation. This creates a situation where an employee cannot shy away from its performance and has to either defend or agree with the evaluation. If the performance is coming out to be below average as per the parameters laid out in PMS, the employee has to provide possible reasons behind it and discuss a plan of action to improve in future with its manager. At the same time, there may be situations where both the employee and manager, in the absence of a PMS, have not realised that the employee is not actively engaged with the organisation or has not proposed any new idea or initiatives. Such insights when produced by the PMS, brings the organisation, the manager and the employee, all three closer to each other and prompt them to engage and thus helps in establishing a correlation between the PMS and employee engagement.

Further, the PMS assists in assessing the employee, their type of personality, attitude, strengths and weaknesses. They may be appropriately deployed to another department, project, or task based on their attributes. This may also help the employee to discover their own strengths, opportunities and ultimately raising the bar of employee engagement. PMS also formally highlights the little accomplishments of the employee, which could be trivial for annual appraisal but may be significant for a quarterly or bi-monthly review performance evaluation. Had it not been PMS, the little accomplishments and unnoticed efforts would have been buried away with time. Therefore, the employee will focus more on their tasks rather than intentionally elucidating work to the manager to gain brownie points. Therefore, an organisation without any sort of PMS is bound to lose a lot.

An organisation without PMS is like sending the test cricket team to play T20 matches and vice versa. For them all 11 can bowl and bat equally.

6. Acknowledging the Manager

Our discussions recognise the job of the manager as most critical and sandwiching in the organisation. Everything the management seeks from the employees goes through the managers; therefore, the position is significant and affects all employees. One thing the manager must never do is act like a post-office and simply pass on the directions to employee and then wait for the work to get completed. An employee expects directions layered with elements such as guidance, effective communication, balanced work distribution, healthy timelines from their manager, otherwise, leads to chaos, stress and anxiety around the workplace and disruption in employee engagement.

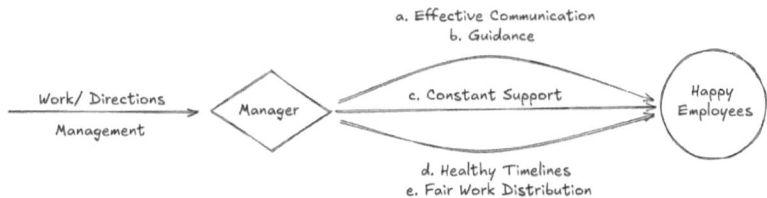

[Fig. 9] Critical role of the Manager

Organisations are not a place for managers and top officials to feel powerful by demonstrating unnecessary authority, but to keep personal ego at bay and organisation's benefit supreme.

6.2 The Manager and its Neutrality

A manager is not only responsible for the development of a project and keeping up with the timelines but also has to manage multiple people to get the work done. We, as human beings, are unpredictable and sensitive, who are still learning about their own behaviour, mind and emotions. We still are very much slaves of our feelings, ego, like-dislikes and moods. These give birth to bias and prejudices which have to be controlled and managed to establish impartiality and neutrality before we start to manage anyone else.

Managers are no different. They were once fresh employees, who gained work experience, skills, degrees and made manager based on their performance. Unfortunately, most organisations miss out on giving emphasis to the important quality of being impartial & neutral as these attributes will assist the manager to get the work done, implement organisational policies, manage employees, reduce attrition with an unbiased and fair minded format. Otherwise, the organisation could lose out on some great human resources. The culture of favouritism not only affects the morale of the employees and work efficacy but also generates waves of negative publicity and erodes organisation's image outside as well.

A bias manager or favouritism around the workplace plays a key role in fostering a toxic environment and employee disengagement. They ruin the efforts of the HR and management towards employee engagement and reduce the utility of implementation of PMS. Once the favouritism begins at the upper levels, it trickles down and spread in various avenues of the organisational structure.

> *"A study found 56% of bosses already have a favourite in mind for promotion before the formal review process, and 96% percent of the time, that favourite gets the promotion."*[22]

6.3 Manager - the Coach

While exercising Performance Management, it should be kept in mind that the periodic one-to-one sessions between the employee and the manager must be organised with a calm and focused approach without any preconceived notions. It should not be treated like the annual salary appraisal discussions. The objective should be to discuss the work progress, impediments, ideas, concerns, and timelines, in short, how we are doing and how we can better ourselves. The sessions should be productive as the time of at least two employees is being invested.

The employee must not just highlight the good parts and accomplishments but also discuss the challenges and present a true picture of the work. The manager should make the meeting accommodating and comfortable for the employee. They must not treat this as an opportunity to criticise the employee for the delay in work, inefficiency and demands put up by them, but ought to raise the morale of the employee.

It is important for the manager to emphasise on their role as mentor to the employee. The main function of the managers and management should be to act as a source of support, an oasis in the middle of a crisis for the employee to recharge themself. Also, as the manager has the advantage of a vantage point above the employee, they should guide, improve and navigate the employee through their workspace by giving correct analyses of their working. Even the best athletes require a good coach, which can see them performing and see what the athlete cannot see. The manager is the coach here.

It must also be noted that the feedback provided by the manager in PMS, should not only be a critical assessment of the performance, but also talk about scope of improvement. To boost up the confidence and trust of the employee, the feedback should be supportive with a personal touch. The employee should receive that the manager has invested its time and given a thought before providing the feedback, as it will give an elevated impression and the chances of the employee taking it seriously and working upon it increases.

7. PMS, HR & Recruiters

With managers, the HR also has a part to play in managing the performance and analysing the working pattern of employees. A manager looks within its team but the HR observes employees across the teams by utilising the reports and data available. The awareness may come through information such as employees in a particular team availing frequent leaves or overtime, irregular login-logout timings or exits coming from particular teams. It is highly possible that due to a toxic manager, the whole team may be suffering and has adapted stress at the job as a new norm.

Managers in order to raise their performance may try to extract more work per employee, often pushing employees beyond a certain limit in terms of workload or time. Sometimes the burden is distributed in the team overall, unfortunately, it also happens that a single employee is overburdened. If such a practice continues for long, the HR should intervene, investigate and address such issues of non-alignment with the standards and policies to the management. Otherwise, the unconducive atmosphere become the new normal and damages the working culture.

7.2 The PMS provides a scanning report of departments which helps in deriving details such as where and how exactly the human resources are invested in, which section is lagging behind with the possible reasons, mismatch between the skill set, pressing needs of the organisation, etc. As the working of the employees are directly reflected, we can say that PMS affects another department in the organisation i.e. Recruitments.

7.3 Recruitments: Whether the organisation outsources the recruitments or has in-house recruiters, they should not only refer to the requirements and remarks provided by the concerned managers but also listens to PMS reports.

The PMS will help organisations derive insights about the skill set mismatch and appropriateness of the talent hired. PMS may also nudge managers to question why they are not able to provide higher ratings to their employees. Therefore, the recruiters will be required to update their approaches, and design of the recruitment strategies. The recruiters may also come to know the gaps in talent expected versus the actual talent hired and what keywords to include and exclude while searching the candidates.

> *"Most valued criteria when selecting early-career hires is potential to grow into a position 83%, critical thinking and emotional intelligence 80%."* [23]

8. Benefits to Organisation

Apart from the standard advantages of having PMS, one of the benefits it offers is uniformity and standardisation in assessing the performance of employees. Organisations with multiple offices at different locations, having the standard operating procedures and parameters laid out in the PMS to be followed by everyone, assists in better deciding the salary appraisals, promotional and other opportunistic aspects related to employees. Therefore, PMS helps in establishing uniformity in performance evaluation and reduces biases. The management will also come to know about engaged and disengaged employees, the sincere ones and the less sincere ones. By configuring this the organisation can actually boost the revenue per employee.

8.2 It is a common scenario to have misinterpretation regarding the development of a task. The manager carries their version of the updates and progress and the employee theirs. Conflicts arise when they confront each other with their versions resulting in trust deficit. Things worsen when such errors in communication are carried long till the annual salary appraisals and affects the remuneration of the employee. In fact, a good percentage of employees would have felt management taking advantage of the occasion of salary appraisal discussions for overly highlighting issues, which could have been discussed and closed earlier. Here, the PMS provides a mechanism to both the employer and employee to attain transparency in identifying and aligning the work with Key Responsibility Area (KRA), goals and timelines. In addition, with PMS, managers and employees will have to consistently interact, evaluate performance, discuss and close the issues. With periodic discussion, both the manager and employee remain engaged in the flow of work on the same page. It also causes the employee to express more about their current functioning in the organisation and future plans and therefore, promotes Employee Engagement.

Majority of the work in an organisation is not rocket science and doesn't not require PHDs to understand and execute. Still, many times the output doesn't come as expected. What we need in organisations is effective communication with distinct and clear directives for the execution of work from top to bottom flow with least ambiguity. In return, the employees should be able to report actual issues with a true picture of the work in a bottom-to-top approach. During this, there should be zero judgments and notions about employees submitting honest work progress.

9. Learning & Development

One of the key takeaways from the outcomes of PMS is the establishment of Learning & Development (L&D) department. When an employee receives low ratings below a threshold in frequent counts, the L&D department may intervene and play a crucial role in finding the gaps and helping the employee improve their performance.

Sample Plan for an Employee Scoring Low in Communication Skills:

Gap Identified: Employee struggles with clear communication during team meetings and is not able to put up their points and thoughts effectively.

L&D Intervention: L&D team may enrol the employee in a communication skills workshop. The team will assign a communication coach for weekly sessions. The workplace will make them practise delivering presentations in low-stress environments with feedback from peers.

Follow-Up: Periodic check-ins to assess progress and offer further support.

By implementing a targeted and supportive L&D strategy, the employee can integrate the necessary skills to improve performance, which will benefit both the employee and the organisation. The skills and learning imparted will also increase the prospects of growth of the employee and thus, raise the engagement of the employee in the organisation's work and business.

An employee is like a rubber band, they can be stretched up as per your requirement, but if stretched too much they will break and will not be useful.

> *From onboarding to performance management system, you have covered a lot. Now we will discuss the right approach towards the exit of an employee in the next chapter.*

*****

"75% of all businesses use exit interviews but only 1% are doing them correctly." [24]

"Out of 150 CHROs of Fortune 500 companies in the fourth quarter of 2023 found that only 10% say their company is highly effective at the "employee departure" stage of the employee experience." [25]

"While 86% leaders believe leadership succession planning is an urgent or important priority, only 14% believe they do it well." [26]

CHAPTER 5
EXIT MANAGEMENT: THE OFFBOARDING PROCESS

The exit process of an employee from the organisation is known as Offboarding. Offboarding is the last phase of the employee life cycle, but an important one. Employee joins a new organisation for delightful reasons such as a better salary, preferred location, brand, roles and responsibilities, etc. They work there and eventually exit in the similar way they had joined from their previous organisation and the cycle continues. Although the exit of an employee is an inevitable process, many times, the employee may not leave with all the happy reasons. Thus, the process of making the exit of the employee, if not all joyous but beneficial for both employee and organisation is called Exit Management.

An employee may leave an organisation for various reasons such as stagnant salary, unfair work distribution, gender discrimination, weak grievance management, thin promotional aspects, ineffective employee engagement, toxic environment, negligible say in the decision making or disturbed work life balance. For almost every such reason, the organisation directly or indirectly is an abettor to the exit of employee.

2. Types of Resignation:

(i) **Voluntary:** The employee submits the resignation due to their own reasons. A formal discussion is held with the line manager, who then discusses the matter with the HR. Therefore, depending on the tasks pending in the team and the rules and regulations of the organisation (such as notice period), the last working day is decided and agreed upon by the employee and the management.

(ii) **Involuntary:** Here, the organisation is compelled to ask the employee to leave the organisation for reasons such as declining performance, retrenchment, restructuring, laying off, etc. The organisation in agreement with the employee asks the candidate to put down their resignation.

(iii) **Termination:** Although not a regular practice, organisations can exercise termination due to unprofessional behaviour or misconduct on part of an employee or gross violation of rules and regulation.

2.2 There could be various reasons for the exit of an employee, but the homework for the management is to introspect how many such exits could have been averted, if they had listened to the employees? How many good, sincere and engaged employees who must have contemplated in their minds, finally chose to leave the organisation? How much does employee turnover cost the organisation? Can we even quantify or monetize the loss of productivity and momentum that the absence of an employee causes, and many more such related questions in concern with the exit management.

3. Exit Interview, a true friend of an organisation:

One of the most important aspects of the offboarding process is the Exit Interview. Every employee during their tenure observes and confronts many shortcomings in the organisation's policies and administration that they didn't disclose earlier. The experiences of an employee exiting can tell us the underlying concerns that we might not be aware of. Such knowledge would be beneficial for the existing employees if the HR and management act upon it. The raw feedback and insights of an employee exiting can prevent many future potential resignations. Is there any discouraging manager making the environment toxic? What made the employee put in the resignation? Are salary appraisals not being conducted regularly and fairly? Are opportunities not being divided equally? Are company policies not serving the purpose? Such are the kind of insights we may get from the exit interviews.

3.2 In our view, it should not be treated as an interview but a candid conversation between the employee and the HR, and may be called anything such as "The Concluding Dialogue or The Final Discussion or The Closing Talk." This is because generally an interview is inclined towards the question-answer format, wherein, both parties play mentally and negotiate with their terms and conditions to achieve their targets. Also, they are not a balanced format or an open-hearted discussion, leading to nondisclosures during the interview which would defeat the very purpose of Exit Interviews.

3.3 For the genuineness and utility of an Exit Interview, the discussion has to be honest. There should be broad titles for the conversation, without restricting it to a set pattern. It is the task of the HR to navigate the conversation without inhibiting the flow of insights coming from the exiting employee. **We have to digest the fact that we can stop an employee from joining the organisation but cannot stop from leaving. We are at the behest and wish of the employee to give us a fair exit interview for the best of the organisation.** Therefore, it is important that the HR make the employee comfortable in sharing information. The management and HR must assure the employee exposing the loose ends during the exit interview that their honest feedback will not impact the experience letter to be issued later and background verification initiated by its next employer.

3.4 Also, in recent times, the value of Exit Interview has climbed up as organisations are understanding the worth of it. The inputs received at every step of the employee life cycle provide a thorough organisation awareness to the CHRO, CEO and other top stakeholders, which are essential for their operations. Also, employee attrition, a concern of the management can be significantly managed utilising the exit interviews.

Therefore, Exit Interview presents a reality check to the management and HR, therefore, is a true friend of an organisation.

4. Listen to the employee leaving

True leaders stand out in the crowd, because they acknowledge, accept and correct if anything had been wronged. In many cases the management and even the line managers see themselves above the organisation and don't want to confront or even discuss the findings of the exit interview. This is a general ill practice across many organisations. Unfortunately, the golden data, proposals and feedback noted during the exit interviews don't see any further light and the company misses out on potential improvements.

This is because the point of actions obtained through exit interviews concerns the management and their policies mostly. In many organisations and majorly in small scale companies, the management is so confident about their present functioning as long as the revenue is being generated that they stop introspecting and valuing the feedback. It is also a reason their growth remains stagnant. **If organisations want to evolve, expand and leave a mark, they have to be bold enough to dive into the sea of criticism (both positive & negative).** We call it hazardous to not take the exit interview and work on the feedback.

> The Key Managerial Personnel and managers should remain humble regarding the organization's functioning, value every resource and feedback, and analyse carefully before rejecting it. Nobody is above the organisation that supports everyone, and its growth should be a shared goal.

5. Employee Lifecycle Fulfilment Index

In continuation of the exit interview process and to understand analytically what the exiting employee intends to convey, it is crucial for the organisations to capture employee satisfaction at various juncture of their tenure.

Employee satisfaction or dissatisfaction originates from the actions of the employer towards the employee. Accordingly, it is becoming important for organisations to assess their current employee related policies and re-aligned them. To make the process effective we have devised the "**Employee Lifecycle Fulfilment Index (ELFI).**"*ELFI works as an index to measure an employee's fulfilment with the organisation's initiatives throughout their life cycle in the organisation.*

This index penetrates deep into the employee engagement efforts of the organisation. Below is a chart for reference, consisting of 9 major parameters, which may influence an employee's work life and decisions the most. In ELFI employees will have to provide ratings out of 10 to each parameter at the time of exiting the organisation and as per their overall experiences during different phases. The parameters and weightage to be designed as per the policies of the organisation.

It is envisaged that the ELFI will provide an insight to the organisation which will help the management and HR come to know areas of concern requiring attention.

Sr. No.	Subject (A)	Parameter (B)	Weightage (C) [total sum 100]	Rating 1-10 (D)	Final Rating D*C/100
1.	Onboarding	1. Overall experience	5	9	0.45
2.	Induction	2. Effectiveness	3	9	0.27
3.	Performance Management	3. Fairness	15	9	1.35
		4. Acknowledgement of efforts	5	9	0.45

4.	Work Life Balance	5. Stress	5	9	0.45
		6. Work distribution/ Overtime	5	9	0.45
		7. Leave availment and policy	5	9	0.45
5.	Growth	8. Internal & Skill Development	5	9	0.45
		9. Professional Growth / Promotions	10	9	0.9
6.	Compensation	10. As per market standards	7	9	0.63
		11. Timely payment	3	9	0.27
7.	Employee Engagement	12. Employee Wellbeing and other engagement initiatives	15	9	1.35
8.	Grievance Management	13. Timely Resolution	5	9	0.45
		14. Neutrality	5	9	0.45
9.	Exit Management	15. Overall Experience	7	9	0.63
		Final ELFI Score			9

#The weightage figures are for illustration only

> *Over-exhausting and burning out employees with stressful and demanding work cultures in exchange for swanky office spaces don't make organisations great. They just save money on employee cost. What qualifies an organisation to stand as an institution is the nurturing and cultivation it provides for the growth and wellbeing of employees and eventually evolves alongside them.*

6. Succession Planning

An important aspect in the offboarding process is succession planning for employees.

When an employee leaves, it not only creates a position vacant, but also delays the progress in the work and affects the team's momentum. There may be critical scenarios where the employee cannot delay their exit, and time-bound tasks may suffer. In such situations, the organisation has to hire a new employee, invest in their training process, and then give them time to get accustomed to the new culture. It is also possible that due to urgency, HR couldn't buy more time and therefore, didn't negotiate much on the salary part and the CTC came to be on the higher side. Similarly, urgency may also cause the hiring of an unfit candidate, which can have a devastating impact on the business, workflow, the team, and begin an intertwined loop of problems.

Thus, an organisation small or big must prepare for such scenarios, and there should be a second-in-command, skilled employee who can compensate and not let the ship sink till the hiring of an appropriate candidate. The succession plans should be part of the culture and must be practised at each level and not restricted to the top designations only.

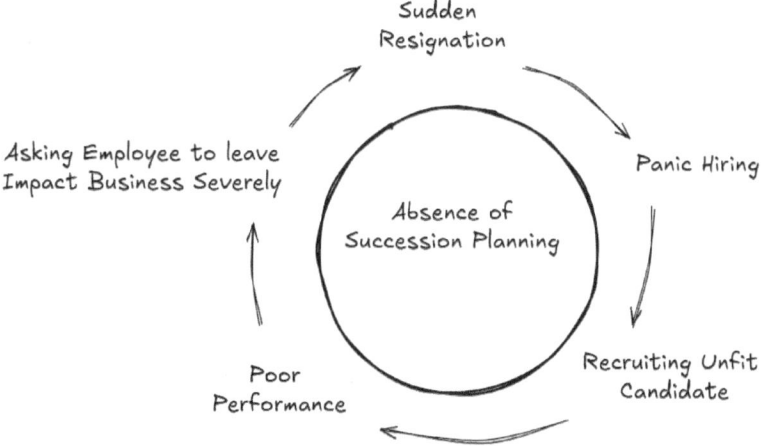

[Fig. 10] Succession Planning

6.2 The organisation exercising the succession plan will also get to know the strength and deficiencies of human capital across different teams and sections. There might be revelation of various kinds, for example

(i) one-sided concentration of experience and skills, that is, the whole team found to be hanging on an individual employee, or

(ii) in an organisation, if the average tenure of employee is around 4 years and the average tenure of employees in a team is found to be 3+ years, then as per the past patterns, this should caution the manager that the probability of employees leaving the organisation may increase, which will create a big vacuum if more than one employee leaves together.

6.3 Further, as the organisation will focus more on flourishing the in-house talent through succession planning, it will benefit on the recruiting costs, time, better success rate, less attrition, and more employee engagement. Accordingly, efforts should also be made on training and development of the employees to bridge up the knowledge and skill gaps as per the requirement of the business and market conditions. Some efforts should also be put in for knowledge rotation of critical tasks among few employees to reduce dependency. In addition, organisations can nurture the existing employees familiar with the work culture, as per the future aspirations of the management. It will allow organisations to strategize and implement things at a faster pace.

7. The Last Day

The last day of an employee keeps the HR department busy in ensuring that relevant NOCs are received from various sections such as IT team for IT infrastructure, accounts section for any due/ surplus funds and final settlement, legal team for any confidentiality agreement, etc. The manager and team members must also remain engaged with the employee leaving, regarding the pending tasks, knowledge transfer, key points and facilitate a smooth exit on a positive note. They must also be sensitive and empathetic towards the exiting employee. A culture may be introduced to acknowledge the work done and achievements of the employee exiting, even if they had not been extra-ordinary.

8. Exit Kit & Memorable Moments

During the onboarding the welcome kit is provided, similarly, the idea of a personalised "Exit Kit" may be introduced including a useful gift or memento as a gesture during the offboarding process. Whenever the article is used or discussed, it will serve as *"Memorable Moment"* in their future lives. The team manager can also maintain a basic timeline and record of *"Memorable Moments"* related to the employee such as achievements, small appreciations, or significant events throughout the employee's lifecycle. Such information may be used during the farewell or other important ceremonies concerning the employee, amplifying its efforts and making the speeches and introductions less generic and more personalised.

9. The Farewell

An employee having worked for your organisation must never leave on an unhappy note. Even if the resignation was put up on a regretful note, it should be attempted that the final day of the employee is different. This is for the sake of the organisation only. By having a warm ending, any hard feelings or resentments can be pressed down substantially. Hence, no employee should leave silently without a farewell ceremony. Also, the exiting employee is soon to become part of the ex-employee community who will present their memories and experiences of the organisation to the outside world.

An organisation as a whole is like a host and mentor to the employee, where the employee learns and grows with good and bad experiences. The employee pays its service, invests its mind and time more than with its family, helps the organisation grow and receives remuneration. This is more than just give and take. Just because there is an abundant supply of job seekers, doesn't make the Exit process and the employee leaving any less important.

Therefore, the positive efforts of the organisation through policies, employee engagement, perks & benefits, HR efforts, etc., must translate into the world and potential joiners knowing and acknowledging that this organisation is a positive and good place to work.

Additionally, it will serve as an example for new joiners to experience the culture firsthand, while also subtly enhancing employee engagement.

10. Ex-Employees

The ex-employee are the graduates of your organisation and will be working across various other organisations at different levels. A professional relationship may be built with them even after their exit through periodic emails regarding job openings, any events of the organisation, sharing any study or research, promotional offer or launch of a product, discounts for being an ex-employee, or any other good deed done at the organisation. This will help in creating a community, where the ex-employee being connected to their past employer will feel less hesitant to rejoin the company or refer a good candidate. An ex-employee having a conversation about the product launch or job position at its ex-employer is nothing but a free promotion. In fact, many big corporations falling under the Fortune 100 such as Microsoft and BCG maintain an exclusive alumni community for ex-employees. [27]

A culture should be envisaged to develop the employee life cycle into an experience and the organisation into an institution. To sum up, Exit is not the end of the employee life cycle but the beginning of recruiting a new candidate and making their life better with the help of past experiences.

*****

Effective Employee Engagement Initiatives

Initiative 01
FREE DAY CONCEPT

Consider an employee working on an idea for the organisation but struggling to find time outside office hours to develop it further. Why should a sincere and engaged employee, who is already dedicating their time and effort during office hours, have to sacrifice their personal time for the organisation's benefit? To address this, a 'Free Day Concept' could be introduced, allowing employees a dedicated day or two to focus entirely on developing their ideas. This initiative could be implemented with prior approval from their manager

Objective

- To promote engagement of the employee in the organisation's business.
- To allow employee to utilise their mental depth and intellect in generating creative and fresh proposals.
- To make employee acknowledge that the organisation values their personal time.
- To boost up employee morale and make them realise that their efforts are recognised.

Initiative 02
UPSKILL

Employees are encouraged to learn and upskill themselves so they can update their professional profile with new skills every 3/4 months. Upskilling can be achieved through online/offline education, technical courses and even reading a significant book related to the core job and presenting the learnings. The organisation should also introduced policies to fund the education completely or at least partially.

Objective

- The employee will utilise the upskilling and learning in the workspace, influencing their colleagues and enabling the organisation to grow along with the employee.
- In the long run, the employee will realise that such employee-focused activities of the organisation helped them grow professionally.
- Promoting and building employee engagement and brand of the organisation.

Initiative 03
HIGH TEA WITH TOP MANAGEMENT

The KMPs (Key Management Personnel) of an organisation should allocate some time to connect with the workforce and discuss what they think of the organisation and how culture, productivity and business can be improved. The conversation could also be about employee background, ideas and its future aspirations, etc. This can be done over a cup of coffee or lunch. The conversation should be frank without the baggage of designations. In the similar way, the managers should also constantly connect with employees under them.

Objective
- To boost morale of the employee and support employee engagement.
- The management will know what kind of a workforce they have and necessary actions to be taken.
- To elevate the employee experience as they can gain insights into the mindset and thought process of the leadership and feel inclusive in the organisation.

Initiative 04
EMPOWER WITH CRITICAL SKILLS

There are some key lifesaving skills such as CPR, basic self defence, application of First Aid, basics of fire-fighting, etc., which everyone should know. Such skills not only save lives but also reduce the intensity of the damage in case a dire event occurs. Unfortunately, very few people know them. Therefore, workshops for these kinds of skills may be conducted

Objective

- The knowledge and application of these skills will not only save lives but will also garner a lot of appreciation to the person. This will also make the employee realise the empowerment and significant development the organisation through the activities have brought into their lives.
- The propagation of the activity by the employee will spread a good name of the organisation.
- The integration of such skills into the lives of employee will promote employee engagement.

Initiative 05
A WEB OF GOOD SAMARITAN

A culture should be established where people at workplace are concerned about each other's well-being. It is even more important in the current times of nuclear family structures.

An employee engagement policy should also include provisions for exceptional cases where medical expenses for an employee or their family exceed insurance coverage and personal financial capacity. In such situations, the employee can submit a request for assistance to the HR Department. If the management finds the medical proposal appropriate and qualifies on a few parameters, it can be floated for a small contribution from each employee towards the cause. In case, an employee finds the proposal moving, they can also connect with the employee for any further assistance. This can be implemented at a global level, where employees of different nations and culture are coming forward to help each other. Similar proposals apart for medical causes, for example, educational expenses, natural calamities or personal tragedy, may also be floated.

The organisation can also create a fund from which some assistance can be provided in the event of such a demanding situation.

Objective

- The activity will help in creating a cohesive culture for all the employees. Employees irrespective of their background will come close for a common cause.
- Employee will take the organisation more seriously leading to an increase in employee engagement.
- Employees can bank upon the organisation and colleagues in tough times.
- Building of goodwill and brand of the organisation.

Initiative 06
LABORATORY

Fostering a culture that encourages open discussions around random yet meaningful ideas, issues, or problem statements. Employees should be motivated to contribute ideas for improving workflows, enhancing processes, and driving innovation. Interested employees from different teams can be invited to brainstorm and collaborate.

Objective

- Employees to utilise their mental capabilities
- Even if they fail, the efforts put in by people strengthens team bonding and new learnings.
- Building a scientific culture to induce innovation.
- It will help in creating a cohesive culture for all the employees.

Initiative 07
DAY OFF FOR FRIENDS

Friends and close family are a part of work-life balance and act as stress busters. Meeting them refreshes us, however, with time, the connections fade away due to various constraints with time being one of the biggest. A policy may be introduced to offer 1-2 days of leave specially dedicated to spending time with close ones.

Objective
- Promoting holistic wellbeing and touching deep into the lives of employee.
- Building of goodwill and brand of the organisation.
- Mental health and stress management.

Initiative 08
REGULAR SESSIONS OF YOGA, HEALTHY DIET, AYURVEDIC CONCEPTS & STRESS MANAGEMENT

We know that practising yoga, stress management, following ayurveda and a good diet are critical to a healthy mind and body. If integrated into our lifestyle, these can prove to be a game changer in our overall well-being. The efficiency at work will also improve if these activities are adopted. However, the time limitations don't encourage one to pursue them. Therefore, this lifestyle can be brought into the lives of employees through regular sessions conducted by the organisation on yoga, healthy diet, ayurveda and stress management and not just once a year to mark the Yoga day.

If feasible, a dedicated practitioner for the above, alongside an allopathic doctor, can be appointed to provide employees with quick counselling on lifestyle and medical-related issues, both for themselves and their families.

Objective

- To improve efficiency and focus of employees by improving their health and mental state.
- To save time and convenience for employees. Such time can be utilised for office work.
- Having such holistic medical and lifestyle-based guidance and counselling facilities available for both employees and their families will have a positive impact on the workforce.
- Feeling of inclusion and employee engagement amongst employees.

Initiative 09
FORMING SOCIAL COMMITTEES & HOBBY GROUPS

Forming social committees comprising employees from different teams to plan and execute employee engagement activities in the organisation. Empowering them to take decisions and bring out new ways to engage the workforce with the assistance of the HR. The committee would also have rotation of employees. In continuation, another initiative that may be undertaken is forming groups based on hobbies such as excursions, art, sports, social work, cycling, dance, etc. This will enable passionate employees to pursue their talents and hobbies within the organisation, with support from the organisation itself. For example: booking a playground for employees who want to play team sports, arranging dance classes and instructors for the dance group, purchasing tickets for movies or plays for the theatre group, organizing an art gallery to exhibit artwork created by employees, or arranging mountaineering activities for hiking and trekking groups.

Objective

- Employees will feel empowered and confident since they have the authority to take decisions and be vocal about their ideas in planning activities.
- The hidden talents of the employee will come out and those who were shy and not engaging will have an opportunity to come forward.
- Employees of different teams across the organisation will get an opportunity to interact with each other.
- Teamwork and employee engagement will emerge among employees.

References

REFERENCES

1,
One third of your life is spent at work, Gettysburg College, https://www.gettysburg.edu/news/stories?id=79db7b34-630c-4f49-ad32-ab9ea48e72b&pageTitle=1 %2F3+of+your+life+is+spent+at+work

2, 4, 5,
State of the Global Workplace 2023 Report, Gallup 3, 23, 2024 talent trends report, Randstad Enterprise

6,
A Great Manager's Most Important Habit by Jim Harter, 30th May, 2023, Gallup, https://www.gallup.com/workplace/505370/great-manager-important-habit.aspx#:~:text=80%25% 20of%20employees,was%20extremely%20meaningful

7,
https://www.tata.com/newsroom/people-first-labour-welfare

8,
26/11 Mumbai attack: HR practices converted ordinary Taj employees into heroes by Saumya Bhattacharya, 24th November, 2011, The Economics Times,

https://economictimes.indiatimes.com/news/company/corporate-trends/26/11-mumbai-attack-hr-practices-converted-ordinary-taj-employees-into-heroes/articleshow/10849491.cms?From= mdr

9, 10,
Employee cost proportion rises for large IT companies by Veena Mani, 27th April, 2023, ET HR World, https://hr.economictimes.indiatimes.com/news/trends/employee-cost-proportion-rises for-large-it-companies/99821706

11,
No call, message after work hours; fines up to ₹53 lakh: New law launches in Australia to protect employees by Sounak Mukhopadhyay, 26th August, 2024, Mint, https://www.livemint.com/news/world/no-call-message-after-work-hours-fines-up-to rs-53-lakh-new-law-launches-in-australia-to-protect-employees-11724672081868.html

12,
Key HR Statistics And Trends In 2025 by Kristy Snyder, Cassie Bottorff & Brette Sember, J.D., 17th May, 2023, Forbes,

https://www.forbes.com/advisor/business/hr-statistics-trends/#sources_section

13,
25 Employee Onboarding Statistics & Trends You Must Know in 2025 by Neelie Verlinden, AIHR, https://www.aihr.com/blog/employee-onboarding-statistics/

14,
Every New Employee Needs an Onboarding "Buddy" by Dawn Klinghoffer, Candice Young, & Dave, 06th June, 2019, Harvard Business Review, https://hbr.org/2019/06/every-new-employee-needs-an-onboarding-buddy

15,
From Capability to Profitability: Realising the Value of People Management, The Boston Consulting Group – World Federation of People Management

16,
These 10+ Onboarding Statistics Reveal What New Employees Really Want in 2023 by Marie-Reine Pugh, 25th January, 2023, Bamboo HR, https://www.bamboohr.com/blog/onboarding-infographic

17,
More Harm Than Good: The Truth About Performance Reviews by Robert Sutton & Ben Wigert, 06th May, 2019, Gallup, https://www.gallup.com/workplace/249332/harm-good-truth-performance-reviews.aspx

18,
Performance Management Benchmarks: PM Strategy, 01st February, 2024, Gartner, https://www.gartner.com/en/documents/5162931#:~:text=Driving%20a%20consistent,in%20PM%20(17%25).

19,
Top 5 Priorities for HR Leaders in 2024, Gartner

20,
2% of CHROs Think Their Performance Management System Works by Ben Wigert & Heather Barrett, 07th May, 2024, Gallup, https://www.gallup.com/workplace/644717/chros-think-performance-management-system-works.aspx#:~:text=Across%20all%20industries%20and%20job%20types%2C%20the%20most%20common%20type%20of%20performance%20goals%20for%20employees%20are%20individual%20goals%20(58%25).%20And%20yet%20managers%20rank

%20team%20and%20customer%20goals%20as%20more%20important%20than%20individual%20goals%2C%20despite%20employees%20receiving%20them%20only%2036%2 5%20 and%2019%25%20of%20the%20time%2C%20 respectively.

21,
The Performance Management Revolution by Peter Cappelli & Anna Tavis, October, 2016 issue of Harvard Business Review, https://hbr.org/2016/10/the-performance-management-revolution

22,
20 Signs of Favoritism at Work and What You Can Do About It, by Michelle Bennett, 20th May, 2021, Niagara Institute.
https://www.niagarainstitute.com/blog/signs-of-favoritism-at-work

24,
Exit Interviews can speak - What can make organizations listen to it? - A Perspective by Seetha Pachchhapur, 09th February, 2024, ET HR World,
https://hr.economictimes.indiatimes.com/news/workplace-4-0/talent-management/exit

interview-can-speak-what-can-make-organizations-listen-to-it-a-perspective/ 107167451

25,
Enhancing the Employee Exit Experience Is Worth It by Corey Tatel, Ph.D. and Ben Wigert, Ph.D., 16th July, 2024, Gallup, https://www.gallup.com/workplace/646937/enhancing-employee-exit-experienceworth.aspx

26,
The holy grail of effective leadership of succession planning, Research report Deloitte Leadership Practice by Jeff Roesnthal, Kris Routuch, Dr. Kelly Monahan and Meghan Doherty

27,
Why Companies Should Stay Connected with Ex-Employees by Geri Tucker, SHRM, https://www.shrm.org/in/topics-tools/news/hr-magazine/companies-stay-connected ex-employees

28,
Why Companies Should Stay Connected with Ex-Employees by Geri Tucker, 19th March, 2018, SHRM https://www.shrm.org/in/topics-tools/news/hr-magazine/companies-stay-connected ex-employees

www.ingramcontent.com/pod-product-compliance
Lightning Source LLC
LaVergne TN
LVHW041614070526
838199LV00052B/3139